The GOSPEL of MARK
LEADER GUIDE

The Gospel of Mark
A Beginner's Guide to the Good News

The Gospel of Mark
978-1-7910-2483-3
978-1-7910-2484-0 *eBook*

The Gospel of Mark DVD
978-1-7910-2487-1

The Gospel of Mark: Leader Guide
978-1-7910-2485-7
978-1-7910-2486-4 *eBook*

Also by Amy-Jill Levine

Entering the Passion of Jesus:
A Beginner's Guide to Holy Week

Light of the World:
A Beginner's Guide to Advent

Sermon on the Mount: •
A Beginner's Guide to the Kingdom of Heaven

The Difficult Words of Jesus:
A Beginner's Guide to His Most Perplexing Teachings

Witness at the Cross:
A Beginner's Guide to Holy Friday

Signs and Wonders:
A Beginner's Guide to the Miracles of Jesus

AMY-JILL LEVINE

The GOSPEL of MARK

A BEGINNER'S GUIDE to the GOOD NEWS
LEADER GUIDE

Abingdon Press | Nashville

The Gospel of Mark
A Beginner's Guide to the Good News
Leader Guide

978-1-7910-2485-7

MANUFACTURED IN THE UNITED STATES OF AMERICA

CONTENTS

INTRODUCTION

In *The Gospel of Mark: A Beginner's Guide to the Good News*, Amy-Jill Levine—"AJ," as she prefers to be called—offers in-depth studies of texts from Mark that she has not covered in her other books. The passages AJ explores are diverse in tone and concerns, but AJ shows how each one challenges readers to discern who Jesus is, for Mark and for themselves, and what the content of the "good news" in this earliest canonical Gospel is.

This Leader Guide will help you lead a small group that studies the stories AJ examines. Its six sessions correspond to the six chapters of her book and include frequent quotations from it. While your group's members will get the most from this study if they have also read AJ's book, this Leader Guide includes enough material for you to engage directly with the biblical text, guided by AJ's information and insights.

Each session in this Leader Guide contains the following elements for you to use as you plan your six in-person, virtual, or hybrid sessions:

- **Session Objectives**
- **Biblical Foundation(s)**—Relevant Scriptures, in the New Revised Standard Version (Updated Edition). This Leader Guide suggests you have one participant (sometimes more) read the biblical text aloud while other participants listen, before reading the text for themselves. You may also want to do two readings: one from the version in this Leader Guide (NRSVUE) or another translation, and one from AJ's relatively literal translation from Mark's Greek text

found in the main book. Participants may reflect on how the different translations impact their first impressions. After each reading, invite volunteers briefly to share their initial reactions before moving into guided discussion. (Session 6 is an exception because AJ's content is structured as a pair of character studies involving several shorter passages.)

- **Before Your Session**—Tips to help you prepare for a productive session.
- **Starting Your Session**—Questions to help you "warm up" your group for discussion.
- **Opening Prayer**—Lead with the prayer provided or one of your own.
- **Watch Session Video**
- **Book Discussion Questions**—These questions can guide you and your group through discussion of each session's Biblical Foundations. You will likely not use all the questions. Choose those you think your group will benefit most from discussing. Or you might formulate questions of your own.
- **Closing Your Session**—You will conclude each session by working as a group on a list of what "the good news" means for Mark's Gospel. As you read each session's stories, participants will add new insights to the list.
- **Closing Prayer**—Lead the prayer provided or one of your own.

Thank you for leading this study! May it lead you and your group not only to a deeper appreciation of Mark's literary skill and theological concerns but also to a richer and more robust life as faithful readers of the Bible.

SESSION 1

The Good News Begins

Mark 1-4

Session Objectives

This session's readings and discussion will help participants:

- Understand some key facts about what makes the Gospel of Mark unique.
- Appreciate why and how Mark uses Scripture to communicate the meaning that ancient as well as today's audiences find in Jesus's story.
- Consider how John's message and Jesus's baptism (Mark 1:1-11), Jesus's call to and table fellowship with tax collectors (2:14-17), and Jesus's parable of the sower and his seeds (4:2-9) can shape beliefs and practices today.
- Begin building your group's working definition of what "good news" means in Mark's Gospel and in their own lives.

Biblical Foundations

The beginning of the good news of Jesus Christ.

As it is written in the prophet Isaiah,

> *"See, I am sending my messenger ahead of you,*
> *who will prepare your way,*

> *the voice of one crying out in the wilderness:*
> *'Prepare the way of the Lord;*
> *make his paths straight,' "*

so John the baptizer appeared in the wilderness, proclaiming a baptism of repentance for the forgiveness of sins. And the whole Judean region and all the people of Jerusalem were going out to him and were baptized by him in the River Jordan, confessing their sins. Now John was clothed with camel's hair, with a leather belt around his waist, and he ate locusts and wild honey. He proclaimed, "The one who is more powerful than I is coming after me; I am not worthy to stoop down and untie the strap of his sandals. I have baptized you with water, but he will baptize you with the Holy Spirit."

In those days Jesus came from Nazareth of Galilee and was baptized by John in the Jordan. And just as he was coming up out of the water, he saw the heavens torn apart and the Spirit descending like a dove upon him. And a voice came from the heavens, "You are my Son, the Beloved; with you I am well pleased."

Mark 1:1-11

Also consider Mark 2:14-17 and 4:2-9 for this session.

Before Your Session

- Carefully and prayerfully read this session's Biblical Foundations—more than once. Consult a trusted study Bible or commentary for background information.
- Carefully read the introduction and chapter 1 of AJ's book. Note topics about which you have questions or want to research further. You might want to keep a record of places where AJ's translation and your Bible translation differ; you can share these differences with the group and discuss what difference AJ's more literal reading makes.
- You will need: Bibles for in-person participants and/or screen slides prepared with Scripture texts for sharing (be

sure to note which translation you are using); newsprint or a markerboard and markers (if meeting in person).

- If using the DVD or streaming video in your study, preview the session 1 video segment and choose the best time in your session to view it.

Starting Your Session

Welcome participants. Tell them why you are excited to study *The Gospel of Mark: A Beginner's Guide to the Good News* with them. Invite volunteers to talk briefly about why they are interested in this study and what they hope to gain from it.

Playfully announce that you have found several fascinating details about Mark. You can ask your fellow participants if they had heard these details before—you can also ask them if the details have any significance.

- Mark is the shortest New Testament Gospel. *Here you might mention famous passages that Mark does not have, from the Sermon on the Mount (that's Matthew 5–7) to the parable of the good Samaritan (that's Luke 10) to the wedding at Cana (that's John 2).*
- Scholars generally consider Mark the earliest written of the extant New Testament Gospels. Most scholars date Mark to ca. 70, after Rome destroyed the Jerusalem Temple in 70 CE. Thus, Mark is writing *after* Paul.
- While early church tradition suggests that "Mark" is the "John Mark" who was Peter's traveling companion, this is probably not the case. You might encourage participants to keep track of how the Gospel presents Peter. In many cases, the presentation is not complimentary.
- Mark contains no stories about Jesus's birth or childhood. *Thus, participants might consider whether a "Christmas" story*

is necessary for the "good news" of Jesus. What if anything does the Christmas story add that is needed?

- Mark also contains, at least in the earliest manuscripts, no stories of Jesus appearing after his resurrection. *As with consideration of Nativity accounts, participants might discuss whether an actual appearance is needed for the Gospel story to be compelling.*

Opening Prayer

Eternal God, you inspired your servant, the one we call Mark, to write the good news about Jesus. May your Spirit now inspire our reading, hearing, and discussion of these ancient words, so they become for us new and living words that make us more faithful followers of the one we call your Son, Messiah, and Lord. Amen.

Watch Session Video

Play the video for session 1. Then ask the following questions:

- Which of AJ's statements resonated with you the most?
- What questions did this video segment raise for you?

Book Discussion Questions

Exploring Mark 1:1-11

Invite a volunteer to read aloud Mark 1:1-11 as other participants listen, Bibles closed. (As AJ notes, Mark was "designed to be read aloud.") You might have another participant read aloud AJ's translation. After the reading, ask participants what most caught their attention—an incident, an image, a word, or phrase—and why.

Invite all participants to turn to Mark 1 in their Bibles and/or share prepared slides. Discuss:

- AJ states Mark's Gospel resembles an ancient biography or "life," written "less to record what happened and more to provide moral guidance." How do you respond to the idea that Mark may be this kind of "life"?

- AJ notes Mark's opening "invokes Genesis" (verse 1). Why might Mark have started his book this way?

- "For ancient Israel," writes AJ, "salvation did not mean an eternal blessed afterlife. It meant salvation from this-worldly dangers...." How could this insight affect our understanding of what Mark means by "good news" (verse 1)? How does this insight affect our understanding of what we think of as "good news"?

- According to AJ, the titles "messiah" (Greek "christ"), "son of god/God," and "lord/Lord" (verse 3) had specific meanings in the ancient world. For example, "messiah" (from the Hebrew, *meshiach*) meant "anointed"; it could refer to a king or even a foreign king, a priest, someone commissioned by God. It did not, outside the New Testament, suggest a divine figure to be worshipped. "Son of God" could refer to Alexander the Great, Julius Caesar, or Hercules. "Lord" (Greek: *kyrios*) could just mean "sir" or it could refer to the divine name in the Old Testament, *YHWH*. What do these various titles mean to you?

- "Understanding ancient texts as referring to something in the present is not a misreading," writes AJ. How do you think Mark understands ancient texts from Malachi (3:1) and Isaiah (40:3-4) to be referring to the story being presented in this Gospel? When have you found new meaning in "ancient texts"—not only Scripture, but also hymns, novels and poems, old movies, and so on—for your present? How, if at all, is that experience like or unlike Mark's "repurposing" of prophetic texts? Why?

- AJ notes that though "classical [i.e., written] prophecy" was believed to have ceased with Malachi, John can be located among the "sign prophets" mentioned by the first-century Jewish historian Josephus. How, beyond his hairy wardrobe (verse 6), do you understand John to be a prophet? Do you think prophecy continues today? If so, whom would you identify as a prophet, and why?

- Malachi anticipated God sending a "messenger"—in Mark's Greek quotation (verse 2), an "angel." "Why look for angels with harps and haloes...?" asks AJ. "There are angels, good-news givers, all around, if we have ears to hear." When has someone been a bringer of good news for you? When have you been one for someone else?

- John baptizes "in the wilderness" (verse 4)—what do you think of when you think of "wilderness" or "desert" (the Greek is the same for both)? Do you recall any Old Testament stories about the wilderness? How might they affect the way you understand Mark's story about John?

- In what wildernesses—physical, emotional, mental, spiritual—do people need to hear good news today? What do you and your congregation do to be "good-news givers" in these wildernesses?

- AJ explains the baptism John practiced was not "anti-Temple protest" but "an invitation for people to repent and then rededicate themselves toward doing what God wants." It is a "public testimony" about personal commitment, accountability to the community, and an indication of the urgency of entering a right relationship with God and others. How is John's baptism like and/or unlike Christian baptism, as your tradition understands and practices it? How, if at all, do you think Christian baptism should be more or less like John's baptism, and why?

- "Repenting means fixing broken relationships," writes AJ, "and so doing one's best to restore community." When have you seen such repentance—or practiced it yourself?

- AJ suggests the "baptism with the Holy Spirit" John anticipated (verse 8) may be "possession" by the Holy Spirit, as opposed to possession by Satan. How do you react to the idea of possession by—or indwelling by—the Holy Spirit? What might signs of such possession be?

- Mark does not suggest that Jesus receiving John's "baptism of repentance" is inappropriate. Do you find Jesus's allowing himself to be baptized problematic? Would AJ's suggestion that Mark's Jesus knows what it's like "to sin, to repent, and to be forgiven" diminish or enhance Jesus in your view, and why? How does AJ's emphasis on Judaism's community-based identity—in which every individual is also part of the community, so that one person's deeds impact the rest of the community—affect your understanding of Jesus's baptism?

- AJ wonders whether Jesus "saw a dove" at his baptism (verse 10) "and interpreted it as a divine message." When, if ever, have you interpreted something in the natural world as a message from God—and how did you respond to that message?

- AJ cites Psalm 2:7, Isaiah 42:1, and Genesis 22:2 as Scriptures Mark may be echoing and "repurposing" in verse 11. These texts can be seen "as pointing to Jesus," she writes, "but they will always have additional meaning.... Anyone can be a beloved child, a suffering servant, a seeker of justice." When and how have you found yourself in one or more of these roles? What about your congregation?

Exploring Mark 2:14-17

Invite a volunteer to read aloud Mark 2:14-17 as other participants listen, Bibles closed. You might have another participant read aloud AJ's translation. After the reading, ask participants to share initial reactions, then turn to Mark 2. Discuss:

- AJ suggests tax collectors in first-century Judea were "the ancient versions of loan sharks and drug dealers, pimps and traitors." Are there certain people with whom you would hesitate associating, or having your children associate with? What do you make of Jesus's table fellowship with people who have harmed the communities in which they live?

- Does thinking of Jesus as "a physician who makes house calls" change your image of him? Have you ever made a "house call" to people who did not know that they were "sick" in the sense of disrupting the community? Is making such a house call potentially dangerous?

- Citing 1 Corinthians 5:9-11, AJ notes Jesus's followers generally didn't continue his practice of eating with "tax collectors and sinners" (Mark 2:16). Were Jesus physically to attend your congregation's next potluck or picnic, would he recognize it as a meal shared with others in his name? Why or why not?

- Why do you think Scripture uses eating and drinking together as a metaphor for the messianic age (as in Isaiah 25:6-9)? When, if ever, have you experienced table fellowship as a foretaste of God's kingdom? How much do you think your congregation's observances of the Lord's Supper (Holy Communion; the Eucharist) express this aspect of the meal's meaning? Are there any other situations, aside from dining together, that you think might be fitting descriptions of the messianic age?

- Why do you think Levi disappears from Mark's Gospel after this story (note his absence in Mark 3:17-18)? How do you and your congregation respond when someone dines with you (literally or figuratively) but doesn't return? If you could write the end of Levi's story, what would it be?

Exploring Mark 4:2-9

Invite a volunteer to read aloud Mark 4:2-9 as other participants listen, Bibles closed. You might have another participant read aloud AJ's translation. After the reading, ask participants to share initial reactions, then turn to Mark 4. Discuss:

- What strikes you about the sower's behavior?
- What do you recall happening to the seed the farmer sows? Why do you think you remembered these details?
- AJ says that "unsettl[ing] everyone," which is what parables can do, is "not a bad pedagogical [i.e., educational] move" on Jesus's part. Have you ever been unsettled when you heard a sermon, read a story, or saw a movie? What made the experience unsettling? Do you think you learned something from that experience?
- Read Jesus's explanation of his parable in 4:14-20. Does this explanation make it easier or harder for you to understand his story? Why?
- Review how AJ's teaching this parable at Riverbend prison reshaped her understanding of it. What might we gain from reading and processing Jesus's parables (and Scripture generally) with others, rather than always only by ourselves? Have you ever heard a sermon or read an interpretation that prompted you to think about a scriptural passage differently? Why do you think you changed your mind?

- As you read and hear this parable today, where and how do you see yourself in it? How might this understanding prompt you to action?

Closing Your Session

In her introduction, AJ explains that what "good news" means for Mark is cumulative: "Mark...offers an invitation: What 'good news' do we find with each story [in his book], and then how do we find 'good news' as we leave the empty tomb and carry the story forward?"

At the top of a sheet of newsprint or on your markerboard or on a videoconference slide, write: "'Good news' for Mark means..." You might start with what you think the good news, so far, is. Invite volunteers to complete the statement based on this session's readings and discussion.

Tell participants your group will continue this project after each session. If meeting in person, keep the list visible for ease of reference during each session.

Closing Prayer

Jesus our Teacher, you went to the wilderness to be baptized, and by your Spirit you enter our wildernesses today, calling us to follow you as you sow your good news. May we receive your gospel with both joy and curiosity, always eager to learn more deeply what it means to us as individuals and as a community, and always desiring to embody it more fully. Amen.

SESSION 2

Restoring Purity and Wholeness

Mark 5-7

Session Objectives

This session's readings and discussion will help participants:

- Understand Jesus's instructions to his disciples (6:7-13) and connect them to their own experiences of evangelism.
- Explore both the picture of worldly power Mark presents in his account of John the Baptizer's death and its relevance today.
- Use the story about a controversy over handwashing in Mark 7 to reflect on the nature of identity-shaping rituals and traditions in their own and their congregation's lives.

Biblical Foundations

[Jesus] called the twelve and began to send them out two by two and gave them authority over the unclean spirits. He ordered them to take nothing for their journey except a staff: no bread, no bag, no money in their belts, but to wear sandals and not to put on two tunics. He said to them, "Wherever you enter a house, stay there until you leave the place. If any place will not welcome you and they refuse to hear you, as you leave, shake off the dust that is on your feet as a testimony against

them." So they went out and proclaimed that all should repent. They cast out many demons and anointed with oil many who were sick and cured them.

Mark 6:7-13

Also consider Mark 6:14-29 and 7:1-15 for this session.

Before Your Session

- Carefully and prayerfully read this session's Biblical Foundations—more than once. Consult a trusted study Bible or commentary for background information.
- Carefully read chapter 2 of AJ's book. Note topics about which you have questions or want to research further. You might want to keep a record of places where AJ's translation and your Bible translation differ; you can share these differences with the group and discuss what difference AJ's more literal reading makes.
- You will need: Bibles for in-person participants and/or screen slides prepared with Scripture texts for sharing; newsprint or a markerboard and markers (if meeting in person).
- This session's discussion of Mark 6:14-29 references child abuse. Be aware this difficult issue may be especially painful for some participants. Be prepared to provide relevant resources and support. (In the US, the Childhelp National Child Abuse Hotline is 800-442-4453 or https://childhelphotline.org/, and the National Domestic Violence Hotline is 800-799-SAFE [7233] or https://www.thehotline.org/.)
- If using the DVD or streaming video in your study, preview the session 2 video segment and choose the best time in your session to view it.

Starting Your Session

Welcome participants. Ask:

- How do you react when you hear the word *evangelism*? (Write participants' responses on newsprint or a markerboard.) Why?
- How much or little does your congregation emphasize evangelism, and why? Does it provide training for people who want to proclaim the gospel, and if so, what kind of training?
- When, if ever, have you risked something to talk to others about your faith? What happened? Would you take that risk again? Why or why not?
- Have you ever found your own attempts to express your faith unwelcome? What did you do?
- Do you think that countries should have the right to forbid evangelism? Would you violate such laws?

Opening Prayer

Holy God, you have always called your people to holy living—proclaiming your mighty acts, bearing witness to your truth, and offering our whole selves to your service. By your Spirit, may these stories of the community Jesus gathered and sent yield new insight into how to live as your faithful people today. Amen.

Watch Session Video

Play the video for session 2. Then ask the following questions:

- Which of AJ's statements resonated with you the most?
- What questions did this video segment raise for you?

Book Discussion Questions

Exploring Mark 6:7-13

Invite a volunteer to read aloud Mark 6:7-13 as other participants listen, Bibles closed. You might choose to read the translation in this Leader Guide, the translation AJ provides, or both. After the reading, ask participants to share initial reactions, then turn to Mark 6. Discuss:

- AJ suggests several reasons Jesus may have sent out his disciples in pairs (verse 7). What are they? What other reasons, if any, might you add?

- AJ discusses Alcoholics Anonymous as one modern example of how the buddy model can change lives. When and how has having a buddy, or a partner, made a positive difference for you or those you know?

- Why does Jesus order his disciples to take so little (verses 8-9)? How do you and your congregation determine what material things, if any, are critical for proclaiming the good news to others? When, if ever, have you discovered something you thought would be important wasn't—or vice versa?

- AJ notes Jesus anticipates his disciples will receive hospitality (verse 10). As she explains, this hospitality involves potential risk and reward for those extending and receiving it. When was a time you experienced hospitality from a stranger? A time you extended hospitality to a stranger? How, specifically, do you and your congregation practice hospitality? How do you discern when hospitality's potential rewards outweigh its potential risks?

- "Lower Galilee in the late 20s experienced no famine or drought," notes AJ. "There was enough to go around."

What do you and your congregation do to help people experiencing food insecurity? What changes would you need to make and actions would you need to take to help ensure there is enough to go around in your community?

- AJ points out the disciples "even supplement Jesus's teaching" by anointing people who are sick with oil (verse 13), which Mark never says Jesus did. What, if anything, might this "supplement" suggest about the roles of adaptation and innovation in faithfully proclaiming good news? What supplements has your congregation or have you personally added in conveying the good news?

- How does this anointing, a tactile, embodied prayer, communicate the gospel in ways words cannot? Are there times when you find human touch to be healing?

- Concerning evangelism: How do we discern which risks we should take, which risks we should not take, and which risks we might not want to take but should?

Exploring Mark 6:14-29

Invite a volunteer to read aloud Mark 6:14-29 as other participants listen, Bibles closed. You might choose to read the translation in this Leader Guide, the translation AJ provides, or both. After the reading, ask participants to share initial reactions, then turn to Mark 6. Discuss:

- AJ states Mark tells this story between Jesus's commission to his disciples and their return (verse 30) to make the point: "Proclaim a Messiah and do deeds of mighty power in his name, and authorities will notice, not in a good way." Have your or your congregation's proclamation of Jesus ever received unwanted attention from authorities? What happened? Would you do anything differently?

- Reread Mark 6:14-16 and then Mark 8:27-29. How does Herod Antipas's confusion over Jesus's identity (verses 14-16) anticipate Jesus's conversation with his disciples at Caesarea Philippi? Based on Mark's first six chapters, who is Jesus to you? What more do you want to know?

- Why do you think Antipas arrested John (verses 17-18)? Why do you think Antipas was interested in what John had to say (verses 19-20)? Have you or someone you know ever been both attracted and resistant to the good news? Why?

- Read Mark 5:35-43, which AJ points out is one of only two stories in Mark "depicting a father, mother, and daughter," the other being the story of John's death. What connections can you make between, and conclusions can you draw from, hearing and reading these two stories together?

- How does Herodias abuse her daughter, and Antipas his stepdaughter? Are you or your congregation involved in efforts to help abused and exploited children? How? If not, what local, regional, or national efforts could you support?

- Antipas makes a rash promise he regrets but keeps (verse 26). Have you ever made a rash promise you regretted? Did you keep it? What happened next? How, if at all, has that experience shaped what promises you make?

- Have you ever done something you knew was wrong to avoid being embarrassed, as Antipas does? What did you learn from the experience?

- AJ suggests that while "blaming the 'evil woman' is an easy and common move," Antipas is ultimately responsible for John's death. Do you agree? Why or why not? How have you seen those in authority in your society exercise power in ways Antipas might recognize? How do you and your congregation respond?

- If you could add to Mark's Gospel, how would you end the stories of Antipas, Herodias, and Herodias's daughter?
- How might John's death anticipate Jesus's death? Can you think of people among the "countless others who have done the right thing, at the cost of their own lives" whom AJ mentions?

Exploring Mark 7:1-15 (17–23)

Invite a volunteer to read aloud Mark 7:1-15 (and, if time permits, 17-23) as other participants listen, Bibles closed. You might choose to read the translation in this Leader Guide, the translation AJ provides, or both. After the reading, ask participants to share initial reactions, then turn to Mark 7. Discuss:

- What traditions and rituals help define your identity? your family's? your congregation's?
- What rituals and traditions would you be surprised and perhaps upset about if you discovered some members of your community did not follow them? What, if anything, would you do about it, and why?
- The handwashing at issue in this story is about "symbolism, not hygiene," AJ explains, because it is a way of "extending priestly privileges to the people"—one of the Pharisees' main concerns. How does this information help you understand their concern regarding some of Jesus's disciples (verse 5)?
- "When it comes to fidelity to Torah," writes AJ, "everyone adapted, since all laws require interpretation." How have you and/or your congregation adapted rituals, traditions, and other practices for new situations? What rituals, traditions, or practices have *not* been adapted that you think should be, and why?

- Why is it important to hear Jesus's response to the Pharisees (verses 6-13) as "insider critique" and not "external polemic" as AJ explains? How has failing to do so contributed to anti-Jewish prejudice?
- Jesus charges some Pharisees with abusing the Corban (*qorban*) system (verse 11), but he does not call for its abolishment. How have you seen positive practices, such as honoring parents or making an offering to God, abused? How do you and your church guard against abusing such practices?
- AJ explains Jesus doesn't abolish Jewish dietary regulations in verse 19 but is making this point: "What is 'permitted' is not necessarily what is 'desirable.'" How do you distinguish between what is permissible and desirable in your life? In the life of the church?

Closing Your Session

Draw participants' attention to the "Good News" list your group began in session 1. Ask, "Based on the stories we've studied today, what else can we say about what 'the good news' means to Mark?" Write participants' responses.

Closing Prayer

Lord Jesus, you did not promise your disciples that following you would be easy. We cannot walk in your way and live in your name without risk. Whether the risks to which you call us seem small or great, may your Spirit strengthen us to take them, that we might show to others and know more fully for ourselves the life-changing love of God. Amen.

SESSION 3

Sacrifice, Ransom, Prophet, Messiah

Mark 8–10

Session Objectives

This session's readings and discussion will help participants:

- Reflect on how our locations (physical and otherwise) shape our perspectives on life, others, ourselves, and God.
- Consider how Mark's story of Jesus's "metamorphosis" (9:1-10) encourages Jesus's followers to look at and listen to him in new ways.
- Discover how Mark's story of Jesus healing a boy possessed by a spirit (9:14-29) challenges understandings of faith, doubt, and belief.
- Articulate ways in which Jesus may have understood his own death, as well as ways in which participants understand his death.

Biblical Foundations

And [Jesus] said to them, "Truly I tell you, there are some standing here who will not taste death until they see that the kingdom of God has come with power."

27

Six days later, Jesus took with him Peter and James and John and led them up a high mountain apart, by themselves. And he was transfigured before them, and his clothes became dazzling bright, such as no one on earth could brighten them. And there appeared to them Elijah with Moses, who were talking with Jesus. Then Peter said to Jesus, "Rabbi, it is good for us to be here; let us set up three tents: one for you, one for Moses, and one for Elijah." He did not know what to say, for they were terrified. Then a cloud overshadowed them, and from the cloud there came a voice, "This is my Son, the Beloved; listen to him!" Suddenly when they looked around, they saw no one with them any more, but only Jesus.

As they were coming down the mountain, he ordered them to tell no one about what they had seen, until after the Son of Man had risen from the dead. So they kept the matter to themselves, questioning what this rising from the dead could mean.

Mark 9:1-10

Also consider Mark 9:14-29 and 10:32-34 for this session.

Before Your Session

- Carefully and prayerfully read this session's Biblical Foundations—more than once. Consult a trusted study Bible or commentary for background information. You might want to compare AJ's translations with the version offered in this Leader Guide: note places where the different translations give you different impressions of the text.
- Carefully read chapter 3 of AJ's book. Note topics about which you have questions or want to research further. You might want to keep a record of places where AJ's translation and your Bible translation differ; you can share these differences with the group and discuss what difference AJ's more literal reading makes.

- You will need: Bibles for in-person participants and/or screen slides prepared with Scripture texts for sharing; newsprint or a markerboard and markers (if meeting in person).
- If using the DVD or streaming video in your study, preview the session 3 video segment and choose the best time in your session to view it.

Starting Your Session

Welcome participants. Tell them that in one story your group will read, Jesus leads three of his disciples up a mountain. Read aloud from AJ's book: "Sometimes, change of location helps encourage new perspectives." Ask:

- Have you ever stood in one place, and then another, and seen the same view but with such a new perspective that it changed the sense of what you saw? What difference did your place make?
- Is there any natural space—mountain, ocean, forest, river, jungle,and so on—that makes you feel closer to God? Why do you think this space makes this impression? Is your experience of God in nature the same as your experience of God in a church or a home or any other building? If so, how?
- When was a time you *unexpectedly* gained a new perspective from being in a different place?
- How can we tell when we need or would benefit from a new perspective about life? others? ourselves? God?

Opening Prayer

God Most High, we honor you as "Most High" and we pray that we remember always that you are also here with us. We ask that you grant us new perspective for this class, by the power of your Spirit—both for our own sakes and for the sake of him who said he came not to be served but to serve, that we may serve him more faithfully, Jesus, Son of Humanity. Amen.

Watch Session Video

Play the video for session 3. Then ask the following questions:

- Which of AJ's statements resonated with you the most?
- What questions did this video segment raise for you?

Book Discussion Questions

Exploring Mark 9:1-10

Invite a volunteer to read aloud Mark 9:1-10 as other participants listen, Bibles closed. You might choose to read the translation in this Leader Guide, the translation AJ provides, or both. After the reading, ask participants to share initial reactions, then turn to Mark 9. Discuss:

- AJ's reading of verse 1 leads her to conclude "the coming of the Kingdom must have been seen by Jesus's disciples." Since neither Jesus's "Second Coming" nor the messianic age have occurred, how might the disciples have seen this Kingdom, if only fleetingly? Have you ever felt the Kingdom as present? When, where, how, and why?
- AJ notes several references to mountains in Mark (3:13; 6:46; 11:22-23). What thoughts and feelings do mountains prompt for you?
- AJ explains that Jesus's miraculously bright clothing would have evoked traditions about both Adam's "garments of glory" (Aramaic paraphrases of Genesis 3:21) and Moses as shining after speaking with God (Exodus 34:29). How do

you understand Adam and Moses? How does comparing Jesus to Adam and Moses add to your understanding of his identity and mission?

- Elijah and Moses are "talking with Jesus" (verse 4), perhaps—as AJ states she likes to think—endorsing and encouraging him "as he now turns toward the cross." Have you ever felt encouraged by people who have a sense of what you are experiencing? Have you ever provided such encouragement to others?

- Mark does not state Jesus replaces either Moses or Elijah. What do you remember about the stories of Moses and Elijah? Why might it be helpful to see Jesus as in continuity with figures from the Old Testament? Given this continuity, do you have different understandings of Moses and Elijah?

- How do Moses and Elijah, like Jesus, "reinforce the affirmation that death is not the last word"? Can you think of any time in your life when you realized that death is not the last word?

- Was there ever a time you, like Peter, were too scared to know what to say (verse 5)? What happened? What lessons have you learned, or could you learn, from the experience?

- Peter's remark is the "earliest literary reference to someone as 'rabbi,'" states AJ. She explains that the term in the first century did not suggest formal training and that "everyone holds the possibility" of being both teacher and student. Who has taught you something important without being a formally credentialed teacher? What qualities made this person's teaching succeed, and how do you emulate her or him?

- For AJ, the cloud (verse 7) evokes not only other biblical clouds (as in Exodus 19:6) but also "dense fogs": "The cloud forces us to see the world otherwise; it heightens our attention." When and how have fog or other weather conditions heightened your attention to the world around you? your attention to God? How could you carry that attention into times of clear weather (literal or figurative)?

- How, specifically, do you "listen" to Jesus (verse 8)? When was a time listening intently to Jesus, in whatever form it takes for you, surprised and challenged you? How did you respond? How does your congregation practice listening to Jesus together?

- Why do you think Jesus commands the disciples to be silent about what they saw on the mountain (verse 9)? When is silence faithfulness? When is it faithlessness?

- Why do you think Jesus calls himself "Son of Man" or "Son of Humanity"? How important is Jesus's identification with humanity/being a part of humanity to you?

Exploring Mark 9:14-29

Invite a volunteer to read aloud Mark 9:14-29 as other participants listen, Bibles closed. You might choose to read the translation in this Leader Guide, the translation AJ provides, or both. After the reading, ask participants to share initial reactions, then turn again to Mark 9. Discuss:

- Mark describes a large, alarmed crowd (verse 15). When, if ever, have you been part of such a crowd? What did it feel like?

- AJ notes Mark uses "alarm" in his book for "times when trust is challenged," and suggests Mark shows that "if we are invested in something," the proper response to alarm is perseverance rather than surrender or flight. When have you responded to alarm with perseverance? When has your congregation? What happened?

- "Whatever we determine regarding the diagnosis" of the boy, writes AJ, "Mark, by detailing the symptoms [in verses 17-18], insists that we pay attention to the suffering both of the child and his father." When, if ever, have you insisted someone pay attention to another's suffering? to your own suffering? What outcomes did your perseverance yield? How, specifically, does your congregation pay attention to others' suffering?

- AJ's translation of verse 17 calls the spirit possessing the boy "a spirit of non-speaking." How do you see "spirits of non-speaking" possessing people in your community or in your own life? Are there times when silence is unhealthy, sinful, even demonic? In such cases, how do you advise responding?

- "Commentators who insist that children were regarded as at best marginalized if not as contemptible misunderstand Jewish culture." How does the father in this story refute such characterizations of Jewish parents? How are you and your congregation involved in serving children in your community who cannot speak for themselves?

- How do you understand Jesus's reaction in verse 19? To whom and about whom is Jesus speaking, and why? How do you respond to AJ's suggestion that "Jesus needed to vent"? How does her reminder that, in Scripture, "accusations of a faithless generation yield to examples of God's loyalty and fidelity" affect your understanding of Jesus's words?

- "It turns out," writes AJ, "we are all part of faithless generations.... We are also faithful, because... faith and lack of faith exist together." In what ways has your generation been faithful to God? In what ways has it been faithless? How does the biblical, communitarian perspective encourage both humility regarding and hope for your generation?

- Jesus tells the father, "All things can be done for the one who believes" (verse 23). How do you react to Jesus's words? How can they be used in helpful ways? How might they be abused?

- AJ calls the father's words in verse 24 "one of the Bible's most profound verses." When has unbelief driven you to call out for help? What happened?

- Do you think that unbelief is the same as doubt? Why or why not? Can doubt lead to deeper belief?

- How do you understand Jesus's private explanation about prayer to his disciples (verses 28-29)? How might prayer help us persevere in working against whatever demons, literal or otherwise, trouble our world, our community, or us ourselves?

Exploring Mark 10:32-34

Invite a volunteer to read aloud Mark 10:32-34 as other participants listen, Bibles closed. You might choose to read the translation in this Leader Guide, the translation AJ provides, or both. After the reading, ask participants to share initial reactions, then turn to Mark 10. Discuss:

- Compare and contrast Jesus's prediction of his Passion (his suffering and death) in verses 33-34 with his earlier predictions in Mark 8:31 and 9:31. Why do you think Jesus changes the details? Have you ever repeated a story but changed the details, and if so, why did you make the changes?

- Read 10:35-44. What do James and John's request and its fallout tell us about the disciples at this point? about Jesus?
- The word *martyr* in Greek means "witness." To what does a martyr's death witness, and how? Review AJ's summary of stories about Jewish martyrs from 2 Maccabees 6–7. How might the history of Jewish martyrs have shaped Jesus's understanding of his own death?
- Read Isaiah 52:13–53:12. How might this text have shaped Jesus's understanding of his death? How did it shape his followers' understanding of his death? AJ mentions other possible identities for Isaiah's Servant. What, if anything, can Christians gain from reading this text as being about someone other than Jesus?
- What understanding of Jesus's death does Mark 10:45 offer? How is its ransom imagery for Jesus's death helpful, or not helpful? What questions about Jesus's death does this metaphor of dying as a "ransom" prompt for you?
- AJ notes Mark uses multiple images for Jesus's death. Which of these other images do you find meaningful, and why? Are there any images or understandings of Jesus's death that you find less or not helpful?
- AJ describes "more generous" and "less generous" ways to understand the "many" mentioned in verse 45. Which of these readings do you tend to agree with more, and why?

Closing Your Session

Draw participants' attention to the "Good News" list your group began in session 1. Ask, "Based on the stories we've studied today, what else can we say about what 'the good news' means to Mark?" Write participants' responses.

Closing Prayer

You call us to prayer, Lord Jesus, that we may share in your work and your witness. Help us to continue to listen to you—in Scripture, in our own hearts, in our relationships with others. Strengthen us to serve you by serving others. And always help our unbelief, that we may grow as your people. Amen.

SESSION 4

Fig Trees and Tenants

Mark 11–12

Session Objectives

This session's readings and discussion will help participants:

- Reflect on their study of Mark's Gospel to this point.
- Consider what lessons, positive or negative, Jesus's cursing of a fig tree in Mark 11 offers for their understanding of Jesus and of the good news today.
- Interpret Jesus's parable in Mark 12 about violence in a vineyard, seeking interpretations that do not reinforce the anti-Jewish bias of many traditional readings.

Biblical Foundations

Then [Jesus] entered Jerusalem and went into the temple, and when he had looked around at everything, as it was already late, he went out to Bethany with the twelve.

On the following day, when they came from Bethany, he was hungry. Seeing in the distance a fig tree in leaf, he went to see whether perhaps he would find anything on it. When he came to it, he found nothing but leaves, for it was not the season for figs. He said to it, "May no one ever eat fruit from you again." And his disciples heard it. . . .

In the morning as they passed by, they saw the fig tree withered away to its roots. Then Peter remembered and said to him, "Rabbi, look! The fig tree that you cursed has withered." Jesus answered them, "Have faith in God. Truly I tell you, if you say to this mountain, 'Be taken up and thrown into the sea,' and if you do not doubt in your heart but believe that what you say will come to pass, it will be done for you. So, I tell you, whatever you ask for in prayer, believe that you have received it, and it will be yours.

"Whenever you stand praying, forgive, if you have anything against anyone, so that your Father in heaven may also forgive you your trespasses"

Mark 11:11-14, 20-26

Also consider Mark 12:1-12 for this session.

Before Your Session

- Carefully and prayerfully read this session's Biblical Foundations—more than once. Consult a trusted study Bible or commentary for background information.
- Carefully read chapter 4 of AJ's book. Note topics about which you have questions or want to research further. You might want to keep a record of places where AJ's translation and your Bible translation differ; you can share these differences with the group and discuss what difference AJ's more literal reading makes.
- You will need: Bibles for in-person participants and/or screen slides prepared with Scripture texts for sharing; newsprint or a markerboard and markers (if meeting in person).
- If using the DVD or streaming video in your study, preview the session 4 video segment and choose the best time in your session to view it.

Starting Your Session

Welcome participants. Tell them your group is now halfway through its study of Mark. Ask them to reflect on the study so far. Offer a reflection of your own to start discussion, and/or use such questions as:

- What about Mark has surprised, interested, or challenged you most?
- What biggest question do you still have from a previous session?
- How, if at all, has our study so far been shaping your understanding of Mark's story of Jesus?

Tell participants this session marks your group's move into Mark's Passion Narrative—the story of the last week before Jesus's betrayal and arrest, suffering, death, and resurrection. Encourage them to keep this background in mind during your final three sessions together.

Opening Prayer

Merciful God, you love us too much to demand unthinking, unfeeling obedience. You command us instead to love you with heart, soul, strength, and mind. As we enter provocative and challenging stories from Jesus's last week in Jerusalem, may your Spirit guide us to receive your word in new ways and equip us to do your will with renewed commitment. Amen.

Watch Session Video

Play the video for session 4. Then ask the following questions:

- Which of AJ's statements resonated with you the most?
- What questions did this video segment raise for you?

Book Discussion Questions

Exploring Mark 11:11-14, 19-26

Invite two volunteers to read aloud. The first should read aloud Mark 11:11-14 and 11:20-25 [26]; in between those passages, the second should read aloud 11:15-19. Other participants should listen, Bibles closed. You might choose to read the translation in this Leader Guide, the translation AJ provides, or both. After the reading, ask participants to share initial reactions, then turn to Mark 11. Discuss:

- As AJ notes, a crowd greets Jesus at Jerusalem as a "conquering king," with "the language of a victory parade" (11:9-10), but Jesus's first actions in the city are quite undramatic (verse 11). How does this development illustrate Mark's "literary art"? What impression does Jesus's lack of direct action in the Temple make upon you?

- Jesus's hunger (verse 12) makes him "cranky," suggests AJ: "Mark forces on the reader the full humanity of Jesus, for better or worse." Do you find a cranky Jesus less relatable or more, and why? In your experience, how eagerly or reluctantly do Christian preachers, teachers, and artists attribute less than appealing but recognizably, fully human feelings and reactions to Jesus? How about you in your personal study and prayer? Why?

- Why do you think Jesus curses the fig tree for being, as AJ writes, "what it had always been, a tree that operates according to the seasons"? Have you ever been tempted to curse something that was doing what it was meant to do, whether from the world of nature or from the world of technology? Did the cursing make you feel better?

- AJ cites several Scriptures mentioning fig trees: Isaiah 28:3-4; Jeremiah 8:13; Hosea 9:10; Joel 1:7; Micah 7:1-2; Zechariah 3:10. Find and read some or all of these "intertexts" (texts related to other texts). After reading the intertexts, do you have a different view of Mark's story of Jesus and the fig tree? Why or why not?

- "Given the sandwiching (intercalation) of the Temple incident between the cursing and the withering of the fig tree, [the scene of Jesus cursing the tree can function] as a parable of judgment on the Temple." Read 11:15-19. Why, in the story, do you think Jesus drives sellers and buyers out of the Temple?

- How is this situation like or unlike that in Jeremiah 7:8-11, which Jesus quotes? How do we understand Jesus's behavior knowing, as AJ notes, both that no historical evidence of corruption in the Temple in Jesus's day exists and that Jeremiah is concerned not with mercantile corruption but with people going through the motions of worship rather than living righteous lives?

- "Some commentators see the story of the fig tree as Mark's way of encouraging readers to pray for [or rejoice over] the destruction of the Temple" in 70 CE. Can you think of any occasions in your own life when you have, or others have, rejoiced over the destruction of property or the loss of life? What dangers does this interpretation hold ?

- What lesson does Jesus draw from "the fig tree" (whether the one he cursed or fig trees generally) in Mark 13:28-31? What "signs" tell you when the time is right for you to repent—in your relationship with God, in your relationships with others—and how do you respond?

- AJ concludes that Mark presents the fig tree story as Jesus's prediction of the Temple's destruction, but the reading bothers her because it suggests "destruction is prompted by sin." What do you believe about God's involvement in destructions and deaths, and why? How, if at all, can or should people acknowledge potentially sinful contributing factors to destruction and draw lessons from destruction? How do you think you and your congregation should respond to destructions, whatever their cause?

Exploring Mark 12:1-12

Invite a volunteer to read aloud Mark 12:1-12 as other participants listen, Bibles closed. You might choose to read the translation in this Leader Guide, the translation AJ provides, or both. After the reading, ask participants to share initial reactions, then turn to Mark 12. Discuss:

- What title would you give Jesus's parable, and why? (*For this question, ignore any titles suggested by your Bible's editors!*)
- AJ doubts the man in the story planted his vineyard or performed the other labor himself (verse 1); rather, she suggests the work was done by "hired or enslaved workers" instead. How does failing to recognize who actually performs hard work, including the work of building infrastructure and cultivating land, lead to injustice? What can people today do to remedy such failures?
- AJ states readers can choose to see the man who planted the vineyard as trustworthy or untrustworthy. What is your opinion of him, and on what do you base it?
- Reflecting on the tenants' possible behavior in their landlord's absence, AJ asks about "the relationship between behavior and oversight." How have you experienced that relationship, as either supervisor and/or one being supervised?

- AJ finds the idea that the tenants stage a "workers' revolution" unconvincing. Why do you think the tenants mistreat and, ultimately, murder the enslaved messengers the landlord sends (verses 2-4)? Why does the landlord continue sending "many others" (verse 5)?
- What do you think of the landlord's decision to send his "beloved son" (verse 6) to the vineyard? "This son is also any person's child sent into battle or sacrificed for a hopeless cause," writes AJ. Does viewing the landlord's son from this perspective change your understanding of the parable? If so, how and why?
- How might this parable encourage people to think about "alternatives other than more death and more destruction" for resolving conflicts? Where do you see people pursuing such alternatives in the world today? in your community? How do or how could you and your congregation support these efforts?
- As verse 12 indicates, Jesus's parable, as Mark tells it, carries symbolic, allegorical weight. As AJ writes, "the chief priests and others recognize themselves as the wicked tenants." Why would Mark make this identification? Do congregations or individuals today hear themselves indicted? Should they?
- AJ suggests we remember "we are all tenants" who "fail to yield what we should ... to God, and therefore we risk our own security." Have you ever held back something from God?
- In allegorical readings, the "Lord of the vineyard" is God. How do you believe God is like and/or unlike the landlord in the story? Why?
- Traditional allegorical interpretations identify the murdered messengers as Israel's prophets. AJ notes few of them, apart from John the Baptizer, were killed. Can you think of any such prophets today?

- "For Mark, the executed [and beloved; compare 1:11] son is Jesus." How is the son's death in the story like and/or unlike Jesus's death? How is it like or unlike the deaths of the enslaved messengers? Do you think some deaths are more important than others: if so, whose and why?
- "The traditional reading...is that the 'others' who receive the vineyard are the (Gentile) Christians into whose charge Israel's legacy...passes." What questions does this reading raise about God's character? How does it relate to such Scriptures as Matthew 5:17 and Romans 11:28-32?
- How does Jesus's quotation of Psalm 118:22-23 (Mark 12:10-11) relate to his parable, as Mark tells it? Outside of this context, what or who else might be "rejected stones" that have become "cornerstones"— in history, in your community or congregation, in your own experience?

Closing Your Session

Draw participants' attention to the "Good News" list your group began in session 1. Ask, "Based on the stories we've studied today, what else can we say about what 'the good news' means to Mark?" Write participants' responses.

Closing Prayer

Before your Passion, Lord Jesus, you sounded challenges that urged all who would hear to recognize the opportune season and appropriate time for repentance and renewal. By your Spirit, you still sound those calls, each and every day. May we welcome your voice, even when we do not fully understand, trusting you will support us as we seek to bear your good fruit and give back what has been entrusted to us. Amen.

SESSION 5

The Little Apocalypse

Mark 13

Session Objectives

This session's readings and discussion will help participants:

- Reflect on people's enduring fascination with predicting the future.
- Understand key features and goals of apocalyptic literature.
- Read Mark 13 closely, analyzing and seeking ethical implications for the present in its apocalyptic imagery.

Biblical Foundation

As [Jesus] came out of the temple, one of his disciples said to him, "Look, Teacher, what large stones and what large buildings!" Then Jesus asked him, "Do you see these great buildings? Not one stone will be left here upon another; all will be thrown down."

When he was sitting on the Mount of Olives opposite the temple, Peter, James, John, and Andrew asked him privately, "Tell us, when will this be, and what will be the sign that all these things are about to be accomplished?" Then Jesus began to say to them, "Beware that no one leads you astray. Many will come in my name and say, 'I am he!' and they will lead many astray. When you hear of wars and rumors of wars, do not be alarmed; this must take place, but the end is still to come. For nation will rise against nation and kingdom against

45

kingdom; there will be earthquakes in various places; there will be famines. This is but the beginning of the birth pangs.

"As for yourselves, beware, for they will hand you over to councils, and you will be beaten in synagogues, and you will stand before governors and kings because of me, as a testimony to them. And the good news must first be proclaimed to all nations. When they bring you to trial and hand you over, do not worry beforehand about what you are to say, but say whatever is given you at that time, for it is not you who speak but the Holy Spirit. Sibling will betray sibling to death and a father his child, and children will rise against parents and have them put to death, and you will be hated by all because of my name. But the one who endures to the end will be saved.

"But when you see the desolating sacrilege set up where it ought not to be (let the reader understand), then those in Judea must flee to the mountains; the one on the housetop must not go down or enter to take anything from the house; the one in the field must not turn back to get a coat. Woe to those who are pregnant and to those who are nursing infants in those days! Pray that it may not be in winter. For in those days there will be suffering, such as has not been from the beginning of the creation that God created until now and never will be. And if the Lord had not cut short those days, no one would be saved, but for the sake of the elect, whom he chose, he has cut short those days. And if anyone says to you at that time, 'Look! Here is the Messiah!' or 'Look! There he is!'—do not believe it. False messiahs and false prophets will appear and produce signs and wonders, to lead astray, if possible, the elect. But be alert; I have already told you everything.

"But in those days, after that suffering,

> *the sun will be darkened,*
> *and the moon will not give its light,*
> *and the stars will be falling from heaven,*
> *and the powers in the heavens will be shaken.*

"Then they will see 'the Son of Man coming in clouds' with great power and glory. Then he will send out the angels and gather the elect from the four winds, from the ends of the earth to the ends of heaven.

"From the fig tree learn its lesson: as soon as its branch becomes tender and puts forth its leaves, you know that summer is near. So also, when you see these things taking place, you know that he is near, at the very gates. Truly I tell you, this generation will not pass away until all these things have taken place. Heaven and earth will pass away, but my words will not pass away.

"But about that day or hour no one knows, neither the angels in heaven nor the Son, but only the Father. Beware, keep alert, for you do not know when the time will come. It is like a man going on a journey, when he leaves home and puts his slaves in charge, each with his work, and commands the doorkeeper to be on the watch. Therefore, keep awake, for you do not know when the master of the house will come, in the evening or at midnight or at cockcrow or at dawn, or else he may find you asleep when he comes suddenly. And what I say to you I say to all: Keep awake."

Mark 13

Before Your Session

- Carefully and prayerfully read this session's Biblical Foundation—more than once. Consult a trusted study Bible or commentary for background information.
- Carefully read chapter 5 of AJ's book. Note topics about which you have questions or want to research further. You might want to keep a record of places where AJ's translation and your Bible translation differ; you can share these differences with the group and discuss what difference AJ's more literal reading makes.
- You will need: Bibles for in-person participants and/or screen slides prepared with Scripture texts for sharing; newsprint or a markerboard and markers (if meeting in person).
- Consider recruiting your volunteer who reads Mark 13 before the session, so the volunteer has time to prepare a thoughtful and meaningful reading of this difficult text.

- If using the DVD or streaming video in your study, preview the session 5 video segment and choose the best time in your session to view it.

Starting Your Session

Welcome participants. Ask:

- Is it possible to predict the future? Why or why not?
- Is it desirable to predict, or to know, the future? Why or why not?
- What comes to your mind when you hear or read about "the end-times"?
- How does your faith or your church experience, shape how much and what you think about the end of the world?

Tell participants they will read and discuss Mark 13 in today's session. You might begin by reminding the participants of these details concerning apocalyptic literature:

- Mark 13 is often called "the little apocalypse."
- *Apocalypse* is from a Greek word that means "to reveal."
- Apocalyptic literature presents revelations about the future in symbolic, "otherworldly" imagery requiring interpretation.
- The future described in apocalyptic literature is known as the "eschaton" (from the Greek term meanings "end") or the "end-times."
- Jewish and Christian apocalyptic literature is found within and outside of the Bible. Major biblical examples include much of Daniel and the Book of Revelation (the book is also known as the Apocalypse of John).
- AJ states, "Apocalyptic literature is designed to comfort its readers by assuring them that God is in control of history, that they are privy to mysteries people on the outside will

never know, that there will be an end to whatever they find oppresses them, and that their fidelity will be rewarded."

Opening Prayer

God who was and is and is to come: We do not know the world's future, or even our own, but believe you are sovereign over all the ages. May your Spirit guide our reading and discussion in this time together, that we may be better able to live today in faithful anticipation of the time to come when your Son, our Savior, will gather us to himself. Amen.

Watch Session Video

Play the video for session 5. Then ask the following questions:

- Which of AJ's statements resonated with you the most?
- What questions did this video segment raise for you?

Book Discussion Questions

Exploring Mark 13

Invite a volunteer to read Mark 13 aloud. You might choose to read the translation in this Leader Guide, the translation AJ provides, or both. Since Mark 13 is very long, you might want to break up the readings into sections, as this Leader Guide also does. After the reading, ask participants to share initial reactions, then turn to Mark 13. Discuss:

Mark 13:1-10

- How do you imagine Jesus's disciples reacted to his prediction of the Second Temple's destruction? Why would some see this event, which happened in 70 CE, as the beginning of the eschaton? Have you ever experienced an event that seemed to you to be "the end of the world"? What, and why?

- AJ asks: "Is there any building, any landmark, without which we cannot live?" How do you respond?
- AJ points out that, because the Temple's Western Wall still stands, "Jesus's statement in Mark 13:2 is partially correct." Have you ever visited this site? What impression did it leave on you? Have other sites left a similar impression?
- AJ suggests Mark 13 may include both Jesus's historical prediction of the Temple's destruction and Mark's own retroactive "prophecy." How much difference does the exact origin of the chapter's content make to you, and why?
- How does Jesus reframe the disciples' question about the timing of the Temple's destruction and what follows it? Why do you think he does not answer their question directly?
- AJ writes that Jesus tells his disciples "to be skeptical of those who claim to speak for him, or as him." When have you been skeptical of someone claiming to speak for Jesus? Was your skepticism justified? Why or why not? What criteria can we use to recognize "false prophets" (see also verses 21-22)?
- Does Jesus's description of wars and disasters as "birth pangs" change how you understand such events? Why or why not? How, if at all, does Jesus's comment that wars and disasters must take place before the end affect his followers' response to the victims of war?

Mark 13:9-13

- "A skinny vanilla latte in a Happy Holidays cup," AJ notes, "is not an eschatological sign." Do you think this alternative to "Merry Christmas" is a sign of persecution or is anti-Christian? Why or why not?

- Where and how are Christians today being persecuted? How do you and your congregation support Christians facing persecution? In your view, does framing disagreements about morals or policies in free, democratic societies as "persecution" help or hurt the cause of people being persecuted for their faith elsewhere?
- Jesus says his "good news must first [before the end] be proclaimed to all nations" (verse 10). As AJ notes, this verse raises questions about proselytism. How do you and your congregation prioritize spreading the Christian message to those who may not have heard it? What forms other than preaching and teaching, if any, do your proselytism or evangelism efforts take?
- Should all religious groups have the right to proselytize in public spaces? Why or why not?
- AJ leaves open the question of whether Jews are "to be proselytized" or whether Jews are "already under covenant." How would you respond to this question?
- Jesus tells his followers not to worry about what they will say at trial. When was a time you wanted or needed to answer someone who was, if not persecuting, challenging your faith? Do you believe the Holy Spirit was speaking through you, as Jesus says the Spirit will? Why or why not? How do we avoid mistaking what we want to say with what God wants us to say?
- Jesus predicts family members will betray each other even to death for fidelity to him. When, if ever, has your faith provoked tension and conflict in your family? How did (or does, or did not) your family manage this conflict?
- AJ says Jesus's words about enduring to the end are "a form of assurance." How assuring do you find them, and why?

Mark 13:14-23

- After outlining various options for what Mark's Jesus meant in referring to the "desolating sacrileg,"/"abomination of desolation," AJ states the phrase is "an open term." What would a desolating sacrilege be in modern terms? Why?

- AJ considers the symbols she sees in houses of worship. Do you know what symbols visitors to your church notice? Has anyone ever asked you about such symbols? How, if at all, might such symbols be understood in ways your congregation does not intend—or even be seen as "an abomination"? Do you think your house of worship uses any symbols it should not, or should at least reconsider? If so, which symbols, and why?

- Some people think placing a state or governmental symbol or flag on the altar or in the church is an abomination; some find it appropriate. What do you think, and why?

- Jesus stresses the unexpected, catastrophic nature of the end-times. When, if ever, has a disaster caught you unprepared? How does that experience shape your response to these verses? How has it shaped your faith?

- "Wars and disasters take a special toll on those who are pregnant and who are nursing infants." How do you and your congregation minister to women in difficult, even life-threatening circumstances?

- AJ says Jesus's mention of winter (verse 18), especially in the context of the end-times, makes her think about climate change. What are you and your congregation doing in response to climate change and to serve those, in your community and beyond, most affected by it?

- How do you think talk of "the elect" (verses 20-22) can be comforting? How important to you and to your church is the idea of an elect group of "saved" people, and why? Do you think believing ourselves to be among the elect helps or hurts our attitudes toward relationships with others? Why?

Mark 13:24-31

- How do you react to the imagery in these verses, which AJ calls "an ancient version of [disaster] movies?"
- As AJ notes, the idea of "the day of the Lord," the beginning of the messianic age, arriving with dramatic heavenly portents was familiar in Jesus's day. How well or how poorly do you think this imagery connects with people in our modern age, and why?
- In ancient people's minds, AJ explains, the world "was alive with supernatural beings, both benevolent and malevolent"—the "powers in the heavens" (verse 25). Do you think this worldview persists even in today's "post-Enlightenment Western world" and, if so, how?
- Unlike other apocalyptic texts, notes AJ, "the coming of the Son of Humanity . . . is about gathering, not about retribution." When you think of the "Second Coming," do you also think of punishment or damnation for the "wicked"? Why or why not?
- Verse 30 echoes Mark 9:1 (see session 3). How do you understand Jesus's promise that his generation wouldn't pass away "until all these things have taken place"? What does the claim that Jesus's words will not pass away (verse 31) mean to you?

Mark 13:32-37

- Jesus says not even he, the Son of Humanity, knows when the end will come. Why, then, have so many Christians (and others) throughout history tried to predict or calculate the end? What dangers might such predictions yield?
- "For Jesus," writes AJ, "the salient question is not the 'when' of the end-time, but the 'how' of living with this expectation." What guidance does his parable (verses 34-36) give?
- What, specifically, does "keeping awake" for the end look like for you? What do you think it means, or should mean, for your congregation?

Closing Your Session

Draw participants' attention to the "Good News" list your group began in session 1. Ask, "Based on the stories we've studied today, what else can we say about what 'the good news' means to Mark?" Write participants' responses.

Closing Prayer

Keep us awake, O God. Save us from sleeping while others suffer. Rouse us from slumber while others cannot rest for hunger or danger or fear. Disturb our tranquil dreams with calls for help from those whose waking moments are nightmares. Keep us awake, O God, and strengthen us for action until the sun and moon go dark and the stars begin to fall at the coming of the Son of Humanity, who will gather your people into the world of which you have always dreamed, even from the beginning. Amen.

SESSION 6

Judas Iscariot and the Naked Young Man

Mark 14–15

Session Objectives

This session's readings and discussion will help participants:

*   Examine Mark's depiction of Judas Iscariot as a way to examine their own responses to Jesus.
*   Wonder about the identity and significance of the naked young man who flees Gethsemane in Mark 14.
*   Reflect on and talk about what they have learned through this study of the Gospel of Mark.

Biblical Foundations

Then Judas Iscariot, who was one of the twelve, went to the chief priests in order to betray [Jesus] to them. When they heard it, they were greatly pleased and promised to give him money. So he began to look for an opportunity to betray him.

Mark 14:10-11

When it was evening, he [Jesus] came with the twelve. And when they had taken their places and were eating, Jesus said, "Truly I tell you, one of you will betray me, one who is eating with me." They began to be distressed and to say to him one after another, "Surely, not I?" He

55

said to them, "It is one of the twelve, one who is dipping bread into the bowl with me. For the Son of Man goes as it is written of him, but woe to that one by whom the Son of Man is betrayed! It would have been better for that one not to have been born."

Mark 14:17-21

Also consider Mark 14:41b-52 and 16:1-8 for this session.

Before Your Session

- Carefully and prayerfully read this session's Biblical Foundations—more than once. Consult a trusted study Bible or commentary for background information.

- Carefully read chapter 6 and the conclusion of AJ's book. Note topics about which you have questions or want to research further. You might want to keep a record of places where AJ's translation and your Bible translation differ; you can share these differences with the group and discuss what difference AJ's more literal reading makes.

- You will need: Bibles for in-person participants and/or screen slides prepared with Scripture texts for sharing; newsprint or a markerboard and markers (if meeting in person).

- If using the DVD or streaming video in your study, preview the session 6 video segment and choose the best time in your session to view it.

Starting Your Session

Welcome participants. Ask: "Which characters in the Gospel of Mark, apart from Jesus, have made the biggest impression on you, and why?" (Tell participants they don't have to pick a character covered in this study.)

Tell participants this final session will introduce them to two more characters in Mark—both of whom remain mysterious, yet both of whom offer us opportunities to reflect on our own responses to Jesus as we consider theirs.

Opening Prayer

God of life and death, your beloved Son Jesus poured out his blood for many and was raised to new life, but too often we respond with betrayal, denial, fear, and silence. May your Spirit lift our minds and hearts to new understanding of and openness to the good news. May the time we spend with Mark's Gospel now make us better readers and especially better disciples, ready to go and tell the story of Jesus of Nazareth. Amen.

Watch Session Video

Play the video for session 6. Then ask the following questions:

- Which of AJ's statements resonated with you the most?
- What questions did this video segment raise for you?

Book Discussion Questions

Character Study: Judas Iscariot

- Mark says Jesus appointed twelve disciples "whom he wanted" to be his apostles (3:13), including Judas (3:19). Mark doesn't indicate whether Jesus knew Judas would betray him. Do you think Jesus knew? Why or why not? AJ asks, "If he did, is Jesus partially responsible for Judas's actions?"—how do you respond?
- Judas is the only one of the twelve apostles identified in Mark 3:16-19 by something he did. Why do you think Mark takes time in 3:19 to identify Judas as Jesus's eventual betrayer? What do you think about Mark and two millennia of his readers remembering Judas only by (to borrow a phrase from AJ's other writings) "the worst thing he ever did"?

- Read Mark 14:10-11. You might choose to read the translation in this Leader Guide, the translation AJ provides, or both. What does the contrast between the way the woman who anoints Jesus uses money (14:3-9) and the way the chief priests in verse 11 plan to use it suggest about faithful and unfaithful spending? How do you determine whether you and your congregation are using money in faithful ways?

- As AJ notes, Mark leaves Judas's motive(s) for betraying Jesus unspecified. What might the notice of Judas's decision to betray Jesus so soon after the story of the anointing suggest? Which, if any, of the other possibilities AJ discusses do you find compelling, and why? Why do you think Mark leaves Judas's motives a mystery?

- Read Mark 14:17-21. You might choose to read the translation in this Leader Guide, the translation AJ provides, or both. Judas appears to be present for the Passover meal and Jesus's institution of what Christians celebrate as the Lord's Supper (Holy Communion, Eucharist). How might remembering Judas's presence at the table move us, as AJ writes, to "examine one's motives before coming to what has become known as the Lord's Table"? How important is moral self-examination for your preparation for Communion? Why?

- Why do you think Jesus, realizing he will be betrayed and by whom, did not tell the other disciples or stop Judas? AJ suggests Jesus should have done so to obey Torah's commandment to "reprove your neighbor" (Leviticus 19:16-17) if you realize your neighbor is about to sin. Do you agree? Why or why not?

- "Was [Judas] following a divine plan?" AJ asks. "If so, then I've got complaints against God." Christians usually

speak of Jesus's death as proceeding, to some degree or
other, according to God's plan; even Jesus apparently
does so (Mark 14:21, 49). To what extent do you believe
Jesus's death was God's plan, Jesus's own choice, the
foreseeable consequences of Jesus's actions—or some of
all three? Why?

- AJ writes, "I wrestle with the idea that anyone is
predestined to do evil." What do you think about this idea,
and why? If such predestination occurs, to what extent,
if any, does it affect the moral responsibility of those who
do something evil? What about those who commit evil
actions arguably because of circumstances beyond their
control such as addiction, mental illness, or economic
circumstances, among others?

- When have you had trouble remembering that someone
who committed evil was created "in the divine image and
likeness," just as you were?

- In Mark, Jesus does not say his blood is poured out "for
the forgiveness of sins" (compare Matthew 26:28). "I
wonder if this addition would have made a difference
to Judas," AJ writes. "I wonder if this addition would
have made a difference to Judas." Do you think Judas
could have been—or perhaps even was—forgiven for
betraying Jesus? Why or why not? Are some acts of evil
unforgivable?

- Commenting on "all" the disciples' promise to not deny
Jesus (Mark 14:31), AJ writes, "Despite promises, we all
fail at some point." When have you broken a promise?
Have you ever thought about such a broken relationship
as you prepare to participate in worship or in the Lord's
Supper? What, if anything, did you or could you do to
make amends for not keeping your promise?

- Judas identifies Jesus to the armed crowd that comes to arrest him by calling him "Rabbi" and kissing him. "Signs of discipleship can be false," writes AJ, "and signs of love can hide acts of betrayal." To what examples in your knowledge or from your own experience can you point of such mis-used signs? How do we keep our own signs of discipleship and love, to Jesus and to other people, true?
- Judas exits Mark's story after verse 45. Why do you think Mark does not tell us what, if anything, happened to Judas? How would you end Judas's story?
- Do you find Mark's silence or the stories about Judas's death in Matthew 27:3-5 and Acts 1:18-19 more satisfying, and why?

Character Study: The Naked Young Man

Invite a volunteer to read aloud Mark 14:50-52, while other participants follow along silently. You might choose to read the translation in this Leader Guide, the translation AJ provides, or both. Discuss:

- AJ calls attention to Mark using the same verb for James and John "leaving" their father to follow Jesus (1:20) and the disciples "leaving" Jesus in Gethsemane. What and who might we need to leave, and what and whom must we not leave, to be Jesus's disciples?
- AJ notes the "young man" (Greek, *neaniskos*) in verse 51 is one of many "unnamed characters" in Mark. Who are the followers of Jesus whose names you don't remember or may never have known, yet who have been important in your story? in your congregation's story? When and why is it important to acknowledge people who are anonymous to us?

- The young man wears only one garment when most people wore outer and inner garments. What might this detail tell us about him?
- The young man's garment is an imported linen cloth. Why might Mark have included this detail?
- AJ says the word for "linen cloth" is the same word for "shroud." What associations does this double meaning prompt for you?
- "Had [the young man] remained with Jesus, also in custody, I would have more sympathy for him," writes AJ. "And yet, perhaps like the Eleven, he represents the future faithful." Do you think Mark expects us to feel positively or negatively toward this young man? Why?
- Review AJ's discussion of the "literary motif of people leaving their garments behind," with Joseph's garment left in the hands of Potiphar's wife as the most prominent example. How might this motif help us make sense of Mark's report of the naked young man?
- "In the presence of Jesus," asks AJ, "are we fully exposed?" When, if ever, have you felt "exposed" before God or Jesus? How did the experience shape, and how does it continue to shape, your faith?
- Read Mark 16:1-8. You might choose to read the translation in this Leader Guide, the translation AJ provides, or both. Mark states the women who go to Jesus's tomb find "a young man [*neaniskos*] dressed in a white robe" there (verse 5). What connections, if any, do you make between this young man and the naked young man in Mark 14? How might these connections change your understanding of both stories?
- What do you think makes the robed young man's message essential for understanding the empty tomb?

- How might 16:7 function as Mark's instructions to those reading or hearing his Gospel?
- "Most biblical scholars agree that the Gospel of Mark ends at 16:8.... The Gospel ends with frightened, silent women fleeing from the empty tomb." Why do you think Mark chose to end the Gospel at this point, without including any Resurrection appearances? What challenges does this ending pose to readers and hearers of Mark's Gospel?

Closing Your Session

For the last time in your study together, invite participants to add to your list of insights into what "the good news" means for Mark, based on the stories studied in this session. Invite volunteers to make any comprehensive statements about Mark's definition of "good news" as they review the list.

Thank group members for their participation in this study. Invite volunteers to talk briefly about what they have gained from it and be prepared to talk briefly about what you have gained leading it. Encourage participants, as AJ does in her book, to continue reading and rereading Mark. Read aloud from AJ's book: "Each time we pass through the Gospel it is not the same, for we are not the same. Each time we are confronted with new mysteries and challenges; each time we find partial answers and temporary comfort."

Closing Prayer

Lord Jesus, you promised to meet your followers in Galilee after your resurrection. We thank you for having met us in our study of Mark's Gospel. We pray you would continue to meet us, by your Spirit's power, as we continue not only to read Scripture but also to respond to you in witness and service. Empower us to make our own proclamations of your good news, in word and in action, as your servant Mark encourages us to do. Amen.

About the
Leader Guide Writer

The Rev. Michael S. Poteet is an ordained Minister of Word and Sacrament in the Presbyterian Church (U.S.A.). A graduate of the College of William and Mary and Princeton Theological Seminary, he serves the larger church as a Christian education writer, biblical storyteller, and guest preacher. You can find his occasional musings on the meetings of faith and fiction at http://www.bibliomike.com.

Watch videos based on *The Gospel of Mark: A Beginner's Guide to the Good News* with Amy-Jill Levine through Amplify Media.

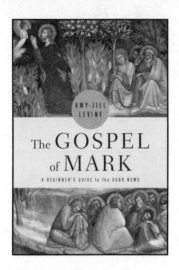

Amplify Media is a multimedia platform that delivers high quality, searchable content with an emphasis on Wesleyan perspectives for churchwide, group, or individual use on any device at any time. In a world of sometimes overwhelming choices, Amplify gives church leaders and congregants media capabilities that are contemporary, relevant, effective and, most importantly, affordable and sustainable.

With *Amplify Media* church leaders can:

- Provide a reliable source of Christian content through a Wesleyan lens for teaching, training, and inspiration in a customizable library
- Deliver their own preaching and worship content in a way the congregation knows and appreciates
- Build the church's capacity to innovate with engaging content and accessible technology
- Equip the congregation to better understand the Bible and its application
- Deepen discipleship beyond the church walls

Ask your group leader or pastor about Amplify Media and sign up today at www.AmplifyMedia.com.